Intrepid Sea, Air & Space Museum

Yankee Stadium
(2.5 miles) →

The Metropolitan Opera House

The Empire State Building

The Chrysler Building

Times Square

Broadway

Central Park

Grand Central Station

The Metropolitan Museum of Art (The Met)

The Guggenheim Museum

Turtle Bay

The United Nations Building

RIVER

Kitty Kat's tour of New York

Kitty Kat, Kitty Kat, where have you been?

I've been to New York, and guess what I've seen...

Russell Punter

Illustrated by Dan Taylor

Kitty Kat, Kitty Kat,
where have you been?

I've been to New York,
and guess what I've seen...

The harbor's the place where my story begins.
The Statue of Liberty welcomed me in.

Next stop, Ellis Island – I went to explore.

It's where lots of newcomers once stepped ashore.

I crossed Brooklyn Bridge to the heart of the city.
You can walk, drive or cycle. It's always so busy.

The One World Trade Center towers up high,
while memorial pools trickle gently nearby.

I rode on the subway that snakes underground.
Over four hundred stations are found around town.

The fine Chrysler Building was built long ago,
designed in a style that they call Art Deco.

The world's biggest station is New York's Grand Central.
It has forty-four platforms – that's quite monumental!

A ship named Intrepid was where I went next.
You'll find lots of aircraft displayed on its decks.

There's a space shuttle too, and a Concorde is here,
as well as a submarine docked by the pier.

Times Square is crowded – folk swarm through the streets.
With its bright lights and billboards, this place never sleeps.

New York's yellow taxis are famous, you know.
I took one down Broadway, where I saw a show.

The Metropolitan Opera House is a fine sight.
Musicians and singers perform there each night.

At the huge Yankee Stadium, baseball is played.
The crowd gives a cheer when a home run is made.

Inside The Guggenheim, great art is found.
Its circular floors twist around and around.

Central Park is the place where the locals have fun.
You can swim, skate and cycle, or go for a run.

There are ball games and horse rides, a grand fountain too,
plus a pond with cute turtles, and even a zoo!

The vast Met Museum has art on each floor,
plus armor and instruments, costumes and more.

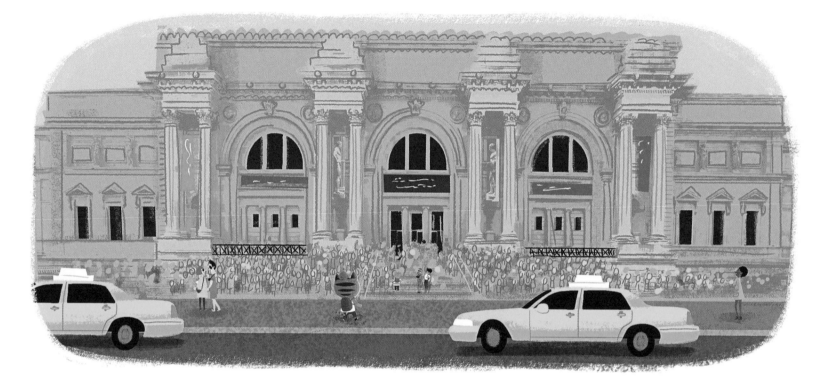

The United Nations is in Turtle Bay.
Nearly two hundred countries hold talks there each day.

The great Empire State Building was my last stop.
One hundred and two floors lead up to the top.

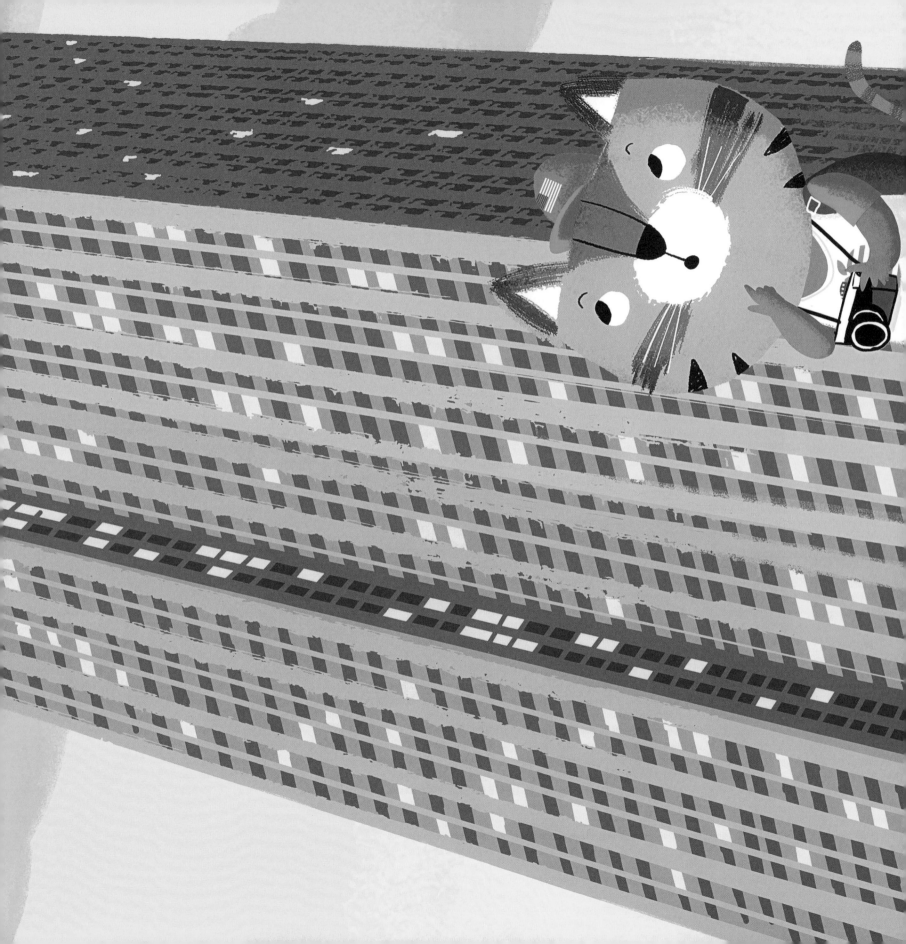

"I'm longing to visit,
since I've heard you talk."

"Well I had the best time.
Now I love New York!"

Edited by Lesley Sims

First published in 2017 by Usborne Publishing Ltd., Usborne House, 83-85 Saffron Hill,
London EC1N 8RT, England. www.usborne.com Copyright © 2017 Usborne Publishing Ltd.

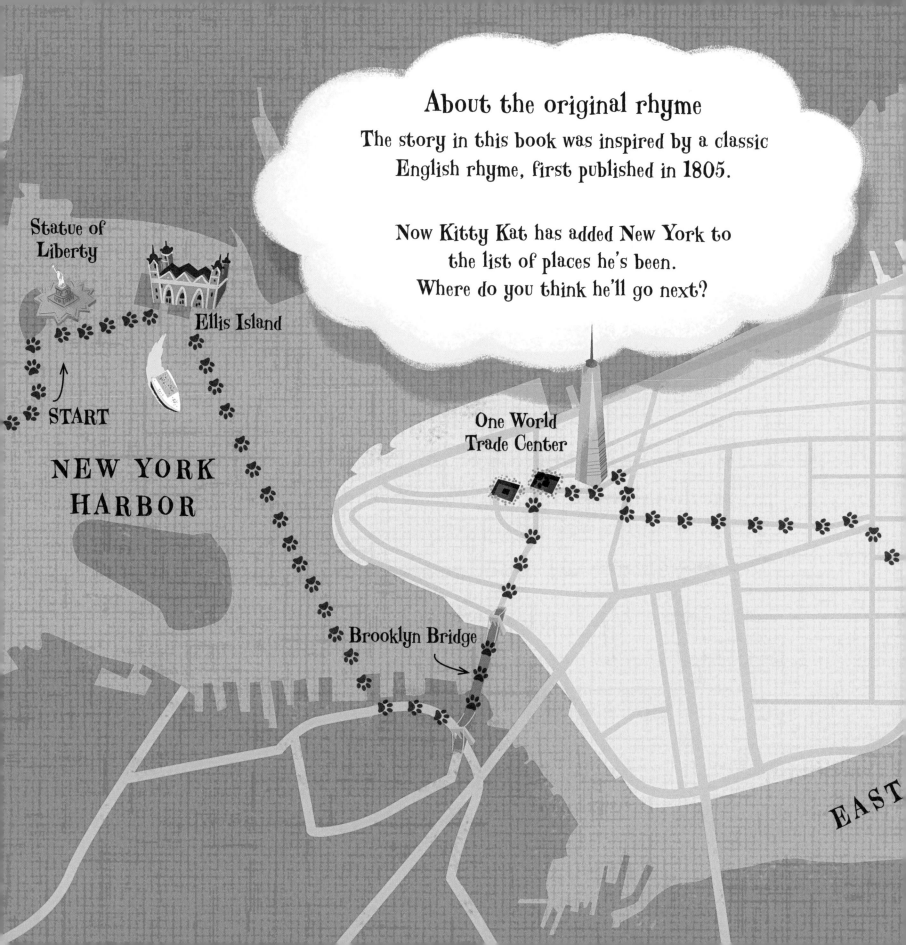

About the original rhyme
The story in this book was inspired by a classic
English rhyme, first published in 1805.

Now Kitty Kat has added New York to
the list of places he's been.
Where do you think he'll go next?

Statue of
Liberty

Ellis Island

START

NEW YORK
HARBOR

One World
Trade Center

Brooklyn Bridge

EAST